THAT'S ANCIENT!

The Innovations of the ANCIENT AMERICAS

BY JANEY LEVY

Gareth Stevens
PUBLISHING

Please visit our website, www.garethstevens.com. For a free color catalog of all our high-quality books, call toll free 1-800-542-2595 or fax 1-877-542-2596.

Library of Congress Cataloging-in-Publication Data

Names: Levy, Janey, author.
Title: The innovations of the ancient Americas / Janey Levy.
Description: New York : Gareth Stevens Publishing, 2022. | Series: That's ancient! | Includes index.
Identifiers: LCCN 2020048542 (print) | LCCN 2020048543 (ebook) | ISBN 9781538265758 (library binding) | ISBN 9781538265734 (paperback) | ISBN 9781538265741 (set) | ISBN 9781538265765 (ebook)
Subjects: LCSH: Indians—History—Juvenile literature. | Indians—Antiquities—Juvenile literature. | America—Antiquities—Juvenile literature.
Classification: LCC E58.4 .L48 2022 (print) | LCC E58.4 (ebook) | DDC 970.01/1—dc23
LC record available at https://lccn.loc.gov/2020048542
LC ebook record available at https://lccn.loc.gov/2020048543

First Edition

Published in 2022 by
Gareth Stevens Publishing
29 E. 21st Street
New York, NY 10010

Copyright © 2022 Gareth Stevens Publishing

Designer: Katelyn E. Reynolds
Editor: Therese Shea

Photo credits: Cover, p. 1 Joshua Davenport/Shutterstock.com; cover, pp. 1–32 (burst) Dawid Lech/Shutterstock.com; cover, pp. 1–32 (clouds) javarman/Shutterstock.com; p. 5 Andrei Minsk/Shutterstock.com; p. 7 (top) Christoph Braun/Wikipedia.org; p. 7 (bottom) Rudolphous/Wikipedia.org; p. 9 Cris Bouroncle/AFP via Getty Images; pp. 10, 11 Yasuyoshi Chiba/AFP via Getty Images; p. 11 (inset) Evgeny Haritonov; p. 12 Thomas Samson/AFP via Getty Images; p. 13 (left) vainillaychile/Shutterstock.com; p. 13 (right) lovelyday12/Shutterstock.com; p. 14 Ernesto Benavides/AFP via Getty Images; p. 15 benjamas11/Shutterstock.com; p. 16 Tobias Schwarz/AFP via Getty Images; p. 17 Ronaldo Schemidt/AFP via Getty Images; p. 18 topseller/Shutterstock.com; p. 19 Christof Stache/AFP via Getty Images; p. 21 Johan Ordonez/AFP via Getty Images; p. 21 (inset) Simon Mayer/Shutterstock.com; p. 23 Robert Michael/AFP via Getty Images; p. 25 Donald Miralle/Getty Images for Lumix; p. 29 (top) Hulton Archive/Getty Images; p. 29 (middle) Mladen Antonov/AFP via Getty Images; p. 29 (bottom) Naawada2016/Wikipedia.org.

All rights reserved. No part of this book may be reproduced in any form without permission in writing from the publisher, except by a reviewer.

Printed in the United States of America

Some of the images in this book illustrate individuals who are models. The depictions do not imply actual situations or events.

CPSIA compliance information: Batch #CWGS22: For further information, contact Gareth Stevens, New York, New York, at 1-800-542-2595.

Find us on

CONTENTS

Ancient Americas 4

Getting from Here to There 6

Ancient Ball Games 8

The Magic Bouncing Ball 10

That's Delicious! 12

Keep a Record of That 20

Add It All Up 22

Stargazing 24

The Great Law of Peace 26

That's Not All 28

Glossary 30

For More Information 31

Index 32

Words in the glossary appear in **bold** type the first time they are used in the text.

Ancient AMERICAS

When do you think the history of the Americas began? Did it begin with the British colonies? Or did it begin earlier, with Christopher Columbus? It actually began thousands of years before his voyage. At least 15,000 years ago, the ancestors of the Americas' native peoples arrived. These early people, called Paleo-Indians, gave rise to great civilizations throughout the Americas. And the many civilizations of the ancient Americas gave rise to numerous innovations.

You're probably familiar with some of these innovations, like the canoe. But did you know that ancient Americans also created the oldest ball game in sports history and that their agricultural innovations have had far-reaching effects on modern diets? Do you like chocolate or popcorn? You can thank ancient Americans for those! Read on to learn more about the innovations of the ancient Americas.

THAT'S FASCINATING!

Just like people did, animals entered the Americas by crossing the land bridge of Beringia. The bison was one of those animals.

BERINGIA

ASIA — Beringia — NORTH AMERICA

EXPERTS GENERALLY BELIEVE THE ANCESTORS OF THE AMERICAS' NATIVE PEOPLES ENTERED THE AMERICAS FROM ASIA OVER A LAND BRIDGE, NOW CALLED BERINGIA, THAT ONCE CONNECTED THE CONTINENTS OF ASIA AND NORTH AMERICA.

The Earliest Americans

Until recently, most experts believed the earliest people in North America entered from Beringia about 15,000 years ago and slowly moved south and east. However, current research has uncovered evidence that people were in North America much earlier. Archaeologists discovered stone tools about 31,500 years old in a Mexican cave. Another study determined that people traveled by boat from eastern Asia to North America about 30,000 years ago. But available DNA suggests the Americas' native peoples aren't likely to be descendants of these people.

Getting from HERE TO THERE

How do you get where you're going? Perhaps you walk, ride a bicycle, or have someone drive you. For long trips, maybe you take a train or plane. People of ancient North America had two choices: walk or use a canoe.

Several canoe types existed. The oldest was the **dugout canoe**, which wasn't unique to North America. Another type of canoe, which was probably invented in southern California at least 1,300 years ago, was built of planks. But the most influential was the birch bark canoe.

Birch bark canoes were invented about 3,000 years ago. They were made of skinned birch bark stretched over a light wooden frame. They were lightweight, sturdy, easy to steer, and quickly adopted by Europeans after they arrived. Modern canoe design is based on these canoes.

THAT'S FASCINATING!

Arctic peoples traveled in **kayaks**, which were invented in Greenland at least 4,000 years ago. In South America, people along the Pacific coast of Peru began using reed boats at least 2,000 years ago.

THESE ARE EXAMPLES OF TWO ANCIENT AMERICAN CANOE TYPES.

dugout canoe

birch bark canoe

What About Horses?

You might be asking, why didn't people of the ancient Americas use horses to get around? There weren't any horses. Interestingly, ancient horses had actually developed first in North America. Some later traveled over Beringia into Asia and spread from there into Europe and Africa. But then the horses in North America disappeared completely around 8000 BCE. The Americas had no horses until Spanish explorers arrived with horses in 1519.

Ancient BALL GAMES

When you think of ball games, what comes to mind—soccer, basketball, football? Those ball games are loved by many, and they've been around a long time. But the world's oldest ball game comes from ancient **Mesoamerica**.

This ball game may have emerged as early as 2500 BCE. The Olmec people probably invented it, although it was most famously played by the Maya and Aztecs. The court for the game had stone walls for sides. A large, vertical stone ring was set high into each side wall.

The game's exact rules are unknown. However, there were two teams of two or three male players, and the aim was to get a solid rubber ball through one of the rings. Hands couldn't be used—only the players' padded elbows, knees, thighs, and shoulders.

THAT'S FASCINATING!

The Mesoamerican ball game wasn't just a game. It often had religious meaning, and the captain of the losing team—or sometimes the entire team—would be sacrificed to the gods!

THESE PHOTOGRAPHS SHOW A LARGE MAYAN BALL COURT. THERE'S A STONE RING NEAR THE TOP ON EACH SIDE.

The Creator's Game

Ancient peoples north of Mesoamerica invented their own ball game centuries before Europeans arrived. The game went by many names, including the Creator's Game, but today it's known as lacrosse. It uses a long stick with a net on the end to handle a ball. The aim is to get the ball down the field and into the opponents' goal. In ancient times, each team might have as many as 1,000 players, goals were miles apart, and games lasted days!

The Magic BOUNCING BALL

Remember the Mesoamericans' rubber balls? They probably don't sound like a big deal to you. After all, rubber is pretty ordinary in the modern world. But it *was* a big deal centuries ago.

Today, we can make artificial rubber. But centuries ago, rubber was only made from the **latex** sap of the rubber tree. This tree grew solely in the warm, wet rain forests of South America. The Olmec, Maya, and Aztecs knew the tree and used its sap to make their balls.

Europeans had leather balls filled with hair, feathers, or air. They were amazed by the rubber balls Spanish explorers brought back. One official at the Spanish court wrote, "I don't understand how when the balls hit the ground they are sent into the air with such incredible bounce."

THAT'S FASCINATING!

You must wait for a rubber tree to reach 6 years of age before you can take the latex sap from it.

THE RUBBER BALLS USED IN THE MESOAMERICAN BALL GAME WERE 4 TO 12 INCHES (10 TO 30 CM) WIDE AND COULD WEIGH 1 TO NEARLY 8 POUNDS (454 G TO 3.6 KG). THEY COULD SERIOUSLY INJURE OR EVEN KILL A PLAYER.

rubber tree sap

From Sap to Rubber

So how did the ancient peoples of Mesoamerica turn latex into rubber? There are theories. It seems likely the people boiled the raw latex with the juice of morning glory vines, which grow near rubber trees. A team of American scientists tried making rubber using these two materials. They found that using equal amounts of the two materials created the bounciest rubber. Using a mix of three parts latex to one part morning glory juice created the longest-lasting rubber.

That's DELICIOUS!

What are some of your favorite foods? You might be surprised to learn how many well-loved foods in the modern diet come from the peoples of the ancient Americas.

Do you like chocolate? Almost everyone does. Chocolate is made from the beans inside the fruit of cacao trees, which are native to Central and South America. The ancient peoples of Mesoamerica invented chocolate perhaps as long as 3,500 years ago. But unlike modern chocolate, their chocolate was a bitter drink.

Do you enjoy corn? The ancient people of Mexico invented it between 7,000 and 10,000 years ago. They **domesticated** a wild grass called teosinte (tay-uh-SIHN-tee). It had **kernels**, like corn, but they were small and not very tasty. By carefully selecting for teosinte's favorable qualities, the ancient people eventually created corn.

THAT'S FASCINATING!

The word "chocolate" comes from the Aztec word *xocoatl*, which was the Aztec name for a bitter drink made from cacao beans.
The scientific name for the cacao tree is *Theobroma cacao*, which means "food of the gods."

TO THE LEFT IS TEOSINTE, THE GRASS FROM WHICH CORN WAS DEVELOPED. IT'S TRULY IMPRESSIVE THAT MEXICO'S ANCIENT PEOPLE WERE ABLE TO CREATE CORN, SEEN ON THE RIGHT, FROM THIS!

Popcorn!

Popcorn is a favorite snack of many people. It's a type of corn, and like all corn, it originated long ago with the peoples of the ancient Americas. In 1948, tiny ears of popcorn were discovered in a New Mexico cave known as the Bat Cave. Those popcorn ears were about 5,600 years old. Then, in 2012, some ears of corn bearing popped kernels were found in the South American country of Peru. Those ears were about 6,700 years old!

Do you like french fries, mashed potatoes, and baked potatoes? Potatoes in many forms are popular parts of the modern diet. If you enjoy potatoes in any form, you can thank the ancient people of the South American Andes mountain system.

Just like corn began as a wild grass, potatoes were once wild tubers. What are tubers? They're short, thick, fleshy stems that form underground. Ancient people living high in the Andes of what's today southern Peru and northwestern Bolivia began domesticating these tubers about 10,000 years ago.

You might be surprised to learn that the potatoes the ancient people were growing—and that you can still find in the Andes—didn't look like the potatoes you're probably most familiar with. They came in different sizes, shapes, and colors.

THESE ARE SOME OF THE DIFFERENT KINDS OF POTATOES GROWN IN THE ANDES TODAY.

THAT'S FASCINATING!

Potatoes are a good source of vitamin C. They lose a lot of it when they're cooked, but leaving the skin on helps reduce the loss.

peanuts

More Popular Food from the Andes

Peanuts are immensely popular as snack food. Perhaps you've heard stories of slave ships bringing peanuts, or groundnuts, to the American South from Africa. That did happen. But peanuts aren't native to Africa. They were introduced to Africa by Portuguese traders in the 1600s. Wild peanuts originated in the Andes of Peru and Bolivia. Ancient people there domesticated the plants at least 7,600 years ago. And later, the Aztecs and Inca mashed peanuts—to make peanut butter!

Do tomatoes make you think of Italian food, with its rich tomato sauces? Well, it might surprise you to learn tomatoes actually originated in the ancient Andes. Tomatoes didn't reach Italy until around 1550.

The wild ancestor of the tomato grew in the high Andes of Peru, Bolivia, and Ecuador. It was a green plant that produced tiny green fruits, which ancient people probably picked and ate. The plant eventually made its way north to Mexico, perhaps by birds dropping seeds. By around 500 BCE, the plant had been domesticated in Mexico.

Experts believe Aztecs were the ones who started cooking tomatoes. Their tomatoes were small and yellow. They called them *xitomatl*. That name eventually became *tomatl*—and that's where we get our word "tomato"!

THAT'S FASCINATING!

Because tomatoes are the seed-bearing part of the plant, they're not vegetables but fruits — specifically, berries. But because they don't contain a lot of sugar, people treat them as vegetables.

Pass the Guacamole!

Do you enjoy Mexican food? Do you like guacamole, the popular Mexican food made from mashed avocado, tomato, onion, and spices? Guacamole was invented by the Aztecs sometime before the 16th century. But avocados have been around *much* longer. Archaeologists have found evidence people in central Mexico were eating avocados about 10,000 years ago. By 5,000 years ago, ancient people in Mesoamerica had domesticated avocado trees.

ANCIENT AVOCADOS HAD A LARGER PIT AND LESS FLESH THAN TODAY'S AVOCADOS.

avocado tree

What's your favorite part of Thanksgiving dinner? Maybe it's pumpkin pie! Pumpkin pie resembling the modern form first appeared in the 18th century. But it wouldn't exist at all if the peoples of ancient North America hadn't domesticated wild pumpkins.

Archaeologists discovered the oldest seeds from domesticated pumpkins in Mexico. Those seeds have been dated to around 5500 BCE. But you probably wouldn't recognize the pumpkins they came from. They were smaller and harder than pumpkins today. And if you could taste one, you probably wouldn't like it. They were more bitter than modern pumpkins.

Why did the ancient peoples grow these bitter-tasting pumpkins? With their thick shell, they survived harsh, destructive weather. Their flesh could be dried and stored for use during long winters or times of shortage.

OVER TIME, BY SELECTING FOR THE QUALITIES THEY WANTED, ANCIENT PEOPLE PRODUCED THE MODERN PUMPKIN.

THAT'S FASCINATING!

You can search high and low for wild pumpkins, but you won't find them. They went extinct about 10,000 years ago!

The End of the Wild Pumpkin

Wild pumpkins may not sound appealing to you. But mammoths, mastodons, giant sloths, and other huge mammals that once roamed North America enjoyed them. These animals could easily break through the hard shell and weren't bothered by the toxic chemicals that produced the bitter taste. They spread the wild pumpkin seeds in their poop. But then ancient people arrived at least 15,000 years ago and slowly killed off these giant mammals. With no one left to eat them and spread their seeds, wild pumpkins went extinct.

Keep a Record OF THAT

You probably do a lot of writing—on a computer, on paper, or maybe on a phone. You may write for school assignments or to communicate with friends or relatives. Most peoples of the ancient Americas didn't have writing systems. But the Maya did. They used their writing system to record events in the lives of Maya rulers and their families.

The Mayan writing system is **complex** and contains over 800 characters, or glyphs. Some are hieroglyphic—that is, they show recognizable pictures of real objects. Others are phonetic, which means they represent sounds.

Mayan writing is hard to understand. A single glyph can represent both a sound and an idea, so it's hard to know how to interpret it. Many glyphs have several meanings. And some glyphs represent several phonetic sounds *plus* an idea!

THAT'S FASCINATING!

Many books using the Mayan writing system existed before the arrival of the Spanish in Mesoamerica. However, Spanish priests destroyed most of them, and only four are known to have survived.

THE MAYAN WRITING SYSTEM BEGAN AS FAR BACK AS 300 OR 200 BCE.

Mysterious Quipu

A quipu (KEE-poo) was an **accounting** device made by native peoples of Peru. It consisted of a long fabric cord with lots of hanging cords—with knots in them—attached. The quipu is mostly associated with the Inca, who flourished from 1400 to 1533, but evidence suggests quipu have been around over 4,000 years. There's also reason to believe quipu were used as a form of writing, not just accounting.

Add It ALL UP

What do you know about number systems? Our number system is **base 10**, and we use Hindu-Arabic numbers. They arose in India in the 6th or 7th century CE and were transmitted to Europe by Middle Eastern mathematicians. But other number systems exist, and the ancient Maya had one.

The ancient Maya used a base-20 system. It's believed this system developed from a tradition of counting on fingers and toes. While our system has 10 distinct digits, their system used only three symbols: a shell for zero, a dot for one, and a bar for five.

We have a place-value system, where the position, or place, of a numeral within a number determines its value. The ancient Maya developed one as early as 400 BCE to 150 CE.

THAT'S FASCINATING!

Experts believe the symbols the ancient Maya used to write numbers represented objects the people might have originally used to count with, such as pebbles, sticks, and seashells.

THIS IS A PAGE COPIED FROM ONE OF THE FOUR SURVIVING MAYAN BOOKS. ON IT YOU CAN SEE WRITTEN NUMBERS.

It's Nothing

How do you know the value difference between 33 and 3,003? It's because of the zeros. In our place-value system, the zeros are placeholders in the hundreds and tens places. They put the threes in their proper places. So the zeros are very important. The Maya had invented zero as a placeholder by 36 BCE. The Mesopotamians had done this earlier. But they were on the other side of the world, and the Maya didn't know about them. The Maya invented zero independently.

STARGAZING

Do you like to watch the moon and stars at night? The ancient Maya are famous for watching the skies. They were great astronomers who studied and recorded the movements of the sun, moon, stars, and planets. Even without tools such as telescopes to help them, they made extremely precise observations. They did all this because they believed celestial events influenced events on Earth. They timed important events on Earth to happen when big celestial events were occurring.

As a result of their careful astronomical observations, the ancient Maya were able to calculate the length of the year to be 365.242 days. The modern calculation is 365.2422 days. They calculated that a **lunar month** is 29.53086 days. The modern calculation is 29.53059 days. The Maya calculations are truly impressive!

THAT'S FASCINATING!

Maya rulers wore symbols of the heavens. They also liked to wear the skin of the large spotted cat called the jaguar because its spots were believed to represent the stars.

THE MAYA OFTEN LINED UP CEREMONIAL BUILDINGS WITH THE SUN. A FAMOUS EXAMPLE IS THIS PYRAMID AT CHICHÉN ITZÁ. IT'S OFTEN CALLED EL CASTILLO, WHICH MEANS "THE CASTLE," BUT IT'S DEVOTED TO THE GOD KUKULCAN, A FEATHERED SERPENT. ON THE TWO DAYS OF THE YEAR WHEN THE DAY AND NIGHT ARE EQUAL IN LENGTH, THE SETTING SUN CASTS SHADOWS ON THE STAIRWAY THAT LOOK LIKE A SERPENT SLIDING DOWN THE PYRAMID. THE SHADOWS END IN THE CARVED HEAD OF A SERPENT AT THE BOTTOM OF THE STAIRWAY.

What Day Is It?

Most people go through life following a single calendar. The ancient Maya used their astronomical observations to create *three* different calendars that they followed at the same time. The Haab calendar had 365 days. It was for ordinary uses like farming. There was a 260-day sacred calendar called Tzolk'in in some places and Chol Q'ij in others. Then there's the Long Count calendar used to date both mythical and historical events. It's 5,125.366 years long!

The Great LAW OF PEACE

What do you know about the Iroquois **Confederacy**? These remarkable people of what is now New York established a **constitution** so impressive that the leaders of the young United States borrowed from it when they created the U.S. Constitution.

The constitution of the Iroquois Confederacy was called the Great Law of Peace. Under this constitution, each Iroquois nation ran its own affairs with a council of elected representatives. But there was also a grand council with representatives from each nation that ran affairs among nations. Members couldn't hold more than one office in the Confederacy. And there was a process for removing leaders if necessary.

If these features of the Great Law of Peace sound familiar, they should. You'll find them all in the U.S. Constitution.

THAT'S FASCINATING!

The Iroquois called themselves the Haudenosaunee (hoh-dee-noh-SHOW-nee). That name means "people of the longhouse."

THE GREAT LAW OF PEACE AND THE U.S. CONSTITUTION

GREAT LAW OF PEACE	U.S. CONSTITUTION
individual nations send representatives to grand council	**Article I, Section 2:** The House of Representatives shall be composed of Members chosen every second Year by the People of the several States **Article I, Section 3:** The Senate of the United States shall be composed of two Senators from each State
members can't hold more than one office	**Article I, Section 6:** No Senator or Representative shall, during the Time for which he was elected, be appointed to any civil Office under the Authority of the United States . . . and no Person holding any Office under the United States, shall be a Member of either House during his Continuance in Office
has a process for removing leaders	**Article II, Section 4:** The President, Vice President and all civil Officers of the United States, shall be removed from Office on Impeachment for, and Conviction of, Treason, Bribery, or other high Crimes and Misdemeanors
asserts who has power to declare war	**Article I, Section 8:** The Congress shall have Power . . . To declare War
admits new nations to the Confederacy	**Article IV, Section 3:** New States may be admitted by the Congress into this Union
creates a balance of power between the Iroquois Confederacy and the individual nations	creates a balance of power between the three branches of the U.S. government: the Congress, the president, and the Supreme Court

Creating the Great Law of Peace

The Great Law of Peace was created in the 12th century in response to a period of constant fighting among the Haudenosaunee peoples. A man known as the Great Peacemaker arrived to bring peace. He had trouble speaking, but with him came Hiawatha to speak for him. Hiawatha presented the Peacemaker's Great Law of Peace. The Haudenosaunee accepted it, and the Iroquois Confederacy was born.

That's NOT ALL

You've read about some extraordinary accomplishments of the peoples of the ancient Americas. But the Americas are vast continents and were home to numerous ancient civilizations. So there were many more achievements than this one book could cover. Here are a few more.

Early peoples of the North American Plains often moved to follow herds of bison, sometimes called buffalo. They invented travois (trav-WAH), which were wooden frames fastened to their dogs by a leather harness, so the dogs could transport their belongings.

There were also housing innovations. An ancient people of Arctic North America called the Dorset were likely the first people to create the snow houses known as igloos. And in the area where Arizona, New Mexico, Colorado, and Utah meet, the people known as the Ancestral Puebloans built amazing cliff dwellings.

THAT'S FASCINATING!

The largest cliff dwelling, located in New Mexico and known as Pueblo Bonito, has 800 rooms!

THESE ARE EXAMPLES OF SOME MORE REMARKABLE INNOVATIONS BY THE PEOPLES OF THE ANCIENT AMERICAS.

igloo ▶

◀ cliff dwelling

dog travois ▶

So Sweet and Juicy!

Do you like pineapples? They're yet one more food we owe to people of the ancient Americas. Pineapples originated as wild plants in the South American countries of Brazil and Paraguay. Native people there domesticated wild pineapples, then took the crop with them as they moved north to Central America and islands between the Caribbean Sea and the Atlantic Ocean. Columbus found the pineapple on an island in 1493 and took it back to Spain.

GLOSSARY

accounting: a system of keeping financial records

base 10: a number system in which each place represents 10 times the value of the place to its right

complex: not easy to understand

confederacy: two or more groups in an agreement of support

constitution: the basic laws by which a country or state is governed

domesticate: to grow for human use

dugout canoe: a long, narrow boat made by hollowing out a large log

kayak: a lightweight boat, often for one person, that moves by paddling

kernel: a whole seed, such as the seeds that cover an ear of corn

latex: a white liquid produced by certain plants that is used for making rubber

lunar month: the amount of time it takes the moon to go around Earth

Mesoamerica: the region that is today the countries of Costa Rica, Nicaragua, Honduras, El Salvador, Guatemala, Belize, and central to southern Mexico

FOR MORE INFORMATION

BOOKS

Englar, Mary L. *The Iroquois: The Six Nations Confederacy*. North Mankato, MN: Capstone Press, 2016.

Green, Jen, et al. *The Encyclopedia of the Ancient Americas: The Everyday Life of America's Native Peoples*. London, UK: Anness Publishing, 2018.

Williams, Brian. *Maya, Incas, and Aztecs*. New York, NY: DK Publishing, 2018.

WEBSITES

Andean and Chavín Civilizations
www.khanacademy.org/humanities/world-history/world-history-beginnings/ancient-americas/a/andean-and-chavn-civilizations-article
Find out about some ancient South American civilizations.

Haudenosaunee (Iroquois) Indian Fact Sheet
www.bigorrin.org/iroquois_kids.htm
Learn more about the Haudenosaunee, or Iroquois.

The Mayas
socialstudiesforkids.com/subjects/maya.htm
Discover links here to learn much more about the ancient Maya.

Publisher's note to educators and parents: Our editors have carefully reviewed these websites to ensure that they are suitable for students. Many websites change frequently, however, and we cannot guarantee that a site's future contents will continue to meet our high standards of quality and educational value. Be advised that students should be closely supervised whenever they access the internet.

INDEX

astronomical observations 24, 25

avocados 17

ball games 4, 8, 9, 11

Beringia 4, 5, 7

calendars 25

canoes 4, 6, 7

Chichén Itzá 25

chocolate 4, 12

cliff dwellings 28, 29

corn 12, 13, 14

Great Law of Peace 26, 27

horses 7

igloos 28, 29

Iroquois Confederacy 26, 27

kayaks 6

lacrosse 9

number system 22, 23

Paleo-Indians 4

peanuts 15

pineapples 29

popcorn 4, 13

potatoes 14, 15

pumpkins 18, 19

quipu 21

rubber 8, 10, 11

tomatoes 16, 17

travois 28, 29

U.S. Constitution 26, 27

writing system 20, 21

zero 22, 23